THE COIN

&

THE STAFF

Ancient Principles for New Age Leadership

UBA ND.

ISBN: 978-978-54635-3-8

Published by U. C-Abel Books
Phone: +23407062756878
Email: *ucabelbooks@gmail.com*

Contents

THE FOREWORD.

THE COIN AND THE STAFF is a unique gift for all today and a legacy for generations unborn. Writing this book is evidence that Uba Nd is passionately committed to driving for Personal Development of his existing and prospective clients as well as leadership improvement. The book discusses the vital issue of Talent and Personal Leadership. Discovering and developing your talents is a critical success factor for living a fulfilled life. It is therefore a must read for all.

I highly recommend it to parents, educators at all levels, coaches and mentors. It is written in a simple language devoid of superfluity which makes it a delight to read. It is an excellent gift for a present.

-Festus O. Azarah

INTRODUCTION

The gift of a man; key to leadership and personal effectiveness.

In our country Nigeria, one of the least discussed topics is the subject of Gift or Talent. It is worthy of note that talent is not celebrated as it ought to be in our nation. Many people are lost when this issue is raised because of misunderstanding and misconception of the subject owing to a lack of adequate study to explain its real meaning. Equally we have failed to comprehend the enormous impact the gift inside an individual can have on him and the society at large.

Understanding, developing and deploying the gift inside of you can raise you from an ordinary person to a person of great influence, obscurity to limelight, poverty to riches and from laziness to effectiveness.

In our society today people of influence are celebrated, recognized, appreciated, admired and respected such that it has become the desire of many to be influential. The sad thing is that the path to becoming a person of influence has not been discovered by many and that is why this book is in your hands to unravel the principles behind it.

The Coin and the Staff? Yes, because the starting point of every human being on earth is not zero but one. Everyone born is wired with great potentials in the inside. The least amount you can ever have is a coin. The particular one you have in your hands is "The Coin". The Coin is symbolic and represents the talent, gift or ability you were born with. You can invest
The Coin and multiply it to billions to the extent that you begin to wield a lot of influence which is what leadership is all about.

The Staff is a symbol of leadership. Remember John C. Maxwell said "Leadership is influence, nothing more, nothing less". There is a vital link between talent and leadership-THE COIN AND THE STAFF. When you discover your talent, develop and deploy it, you will receive the Staff of leadership.
Understanding this link will make you successful and bring out the leader in you.

Lack of understanding of this is the reason lots of people in business or work today are engaged in a futile struggle to make it in life. They are putting in a lot of effort and yet having very little success. They are frustrated because it's just not working for them. Reason being that the business or work they are doing is as a result of parental pressure, peer pressure or what they feel is the happening kind of business or work. These same people, if redirected to put in the same effort in their area of talent, will suddenly come alive and begin to experience success. We have forgotten that discovering your talent and building your work around it is the key to job satisfaction. You excel easily at things you are good at because you were wired to do that. What you are good at is your talent.

Discovering your talent early in life and focusing on it is the secret of success of many great leaders in different spheres of life - be it sports, business, entertainment, education, politics, social etc. It is what has made the difference so far between us and the developed countries. Little wonder why despite having the world's 7 largest population (170,123,000) our nation cannot boast of ranking among the best in producing great talented people in the various spheres of influence. The same is not the case for developed countries. They celebrate talent to the highest level. They focus on early discoveries, development and deployment of talent and place a demand on a high level of excellence. This is why you can hardly find mediocres handling lofty positions in developed countries.

Parents and primary school teachers ought to be properly educated, and seminars held to train them on the subject of discovering gifts/talents of children. Reason being that they are responsible for the early development of a child. If our society can focus on this, encourage these children to strive towards excellence and strategically deploy them in service to our nation, our country will be rid of mediocrity. This is because there are several people in positions in our nation who are not talented and have no passion for what they are doing, and are not committed to excellence.

It has been discovered that the key to excellent performance is finding the match between your talents and your role. This means to a large extent that you cannot be the best or excel in any area where you are not gifted. It is also true that your easiest and most effective path to success is developing and deploying your gift. Diligence in your gift will bring you before great people.

This book "The Coin and the Staff" will give you a good understanding of what talent is. Equally it has the purpose of helping you discover your talent and gift and proffer practical ways on how you can become a leader in that area thereby becoming effective, influential and successful. This will make you relevant and useful to your society. It's a practical book which will require a lot of self-discipline from you to do all that is needful for your success. In this book, the words talent and gift will be used interchangeably because they mean the same thing.

I guarantee that you will become a great leader in your generation if you practise what you will learn from this book.

1

UNDERSTANDING GIFTS/TALENTS

"Any fool can know. The point is to understand."
— Albert Einstein

The reason our nation and a lot of people are not paying attention to the subject of talent is hinged on the misconception of the topic. We do not understand that part of the solution to our problem is to comprehend and educate people on The Coin and The Staff. They do not have the slightest understanding of what talent or gift is, and a lack of understanding of any subject is the beginning of failure.

W. Clement Stone wrote that "truth will always be truth, regardless of lack of understanding, disbelief or ignorance."

Misconception can be defined as a false or mistaken view or opinion about something. This is the case whenever the subject of talent is discussed. It is important to note that many people don't see themselves as talented because whenever the issue of talent is discussed, they only think in terms of singing, dancing, acting, playing musical instruments and sports.

Anything outside of this for people is not seen as a gift or talent. For them, talent starts and ends with the above mentioned list. They see themselves as not possessing any talent at all once they can't do any of the things listed above. This is a very disturbing situation that has robbed individuals and our nation of greatness. A lot of talents are wasting and rotting away. This is why most Reality TV talent discovery programs in our nation are all about singing, dancing, and comedy. A low percentage of our population possess these qualities mentioned above, while the larger percentage does not. That is why whenever you discuss issues about being

> *"truth will always be truth, regardless of lack of understanding, disbelief or ignorance."*
> W. Clement Stone

talented, they shut out, feeling that they are not involved. Recently, a church organized a talent hunt discovery program for singers; a young lady walked up to me and said, "the program is not for people like us who are not talented". I was also speaking somewhere on this topic and a lady stood up and said "my problem is that I do not have any gift but I know how to cook". For her, knowing how to cook is not a gift. What a misconception! We will look into what talents really are with a view to correcting these misconceptions and lay a good foundation of understanding what talents really are.

For us to have a clear grasp of what talent is, it is important to define it. Talent is a natural endowment or ability of superior quality. It is also an innate ability. Innate in the sense that it is inherent, meaning you were born with it. It is a gift, you did not acquire it. Talent can also mean the skill that someone displays quite naturally while doing something that is otherwise hard for other people. Someone who has talent is able to do something without trying hard. It is a high degree of ability or of aptitude. Though some people look at talent as a skill that can be acquired, we are looking at it from the perspective of what you have possessed from birth. God in the process of creating you imputed it as part of your make-up.

Someone who has talent is talented and a talented person is a gifted person.

For further understanding, Marcus Buckingham and Curt W. Coffman after series of study, in their article SELECTING TALENT FIRST, defined talent as ' a recurring pattern of thought, feeling or behaviour that can be productively applied'.

"Every role performed at excellence, requires talent, because it requires certain recurring patterns of thought or feeling".
Marcus Buckingham & Curt W. Coffman

The emphasis here is recurring, meaning that your gifts or talents are the behaviours you find yourself exhibiting often, or the thoughts or feelings you have often. This shows that everyone has a mental filter that sifts through our world, forcing us to pay attention to some stimuli, while others slip past us unnoticed. We just find ourselves repeatedly doing certain things more often than others. They also put it this way, "every role performed at excellence, requires talent, because it requires certain recurring patterns of thought or feeling". The emphasis in this is 'every role'. This means an excellent driver, architect, engineer, nurse, carpenter, teacher, banker, shoemaker, hair dresser, doctor etc., who displays exceptional ability in the discharge of his/her duties is talented or gifted.

In addition, your distinctive ability to remember faces more than names or vice versa, as little as they sound, is talent. Even your ability to constantly flash a radiant smile is a gift. Note that talent is not just any ability you have to get something done, it is a unique special ability you have. The fact is that you have so many abilities, but there is one or more that comes easily to you and is unique and special. That indeed is a talent you have.

Our God, creator and manufacturer who is omniscient and is the epitome of wisdom also gave us an insight which can help us understand the subject of talent. From the book of Exodus in the Bible, when it was time to build the Tabernacle and the Ark of the Covenant, God said to Moses in Exodus chapter 31 from verse 2

"Look, I have chosen Bezalel son of Uri, grandson of Hur, of the tribe of Judah. I have filled him with the Spirit of God, giving him great wisdom, intelligence, and skill in all kinds of craft. He is able to create beautiful objects from gold, silver, and bronze. He is skilled in cutting and setting gemstones and in carving wood. Yes, he is a master at every craft! And I have appointed Oholiab son of Ahisamach, of the tribe of Dan , to be his assistant .Moreover, I have given special skill to all the

naturally talented craftsmen so they can make all the things I have instructed you to make" Exodus 31:2-6(NLT).

Also in Exodus Chapter 35 verse 34-35(NLT)

"And the Lord has given both him and Oholiab son of Dan, the ability to teach their skills to others. The Lord has given them special skills as jewelers, designers, weavers, and embroiders in blue, purple, and scarlet yarn on fine linen cloth. They excel in all the crafts needed for the work".

Many things can be deduced from these verses of scripture, but our emphases here are two things:
1. God made it clear that He gives different gifts in different areas as He wills.

2. Talents are not just about singing, dancing etc. but that you can be talented as a carpenter, hair dresser, jeweler, weaver, lawyer etc.

We also discovered that God gave Oholiab, the ability to teach. This means that you can be a talented teacher or lecturer. In conclusion, the subject of talent is not limited, but cuts across every endeavour of life.

There are about eight spheres of influence that govern

our world. Your talent/gift falls into one or more of these spheres.

1. **World of Politics:** This deals with the activity concerning acquisition or exercising of power within a group or organization.

2. **World of Entertainment:** This concerns the act or process of providing something interesting or enjoyable for someone.

> *"Discovering your talent early in one or more of these spheres of life, nurturing, developing and engaging it is key to your leadership development, becoming influential and successful in life."*

3. **World of Sports:** This is about an individual or group activity pursued for exercise, competition or pleasure.

4. **World of Education:** This deals with the process of imparting knowledge.

5. **World of Arts and Culture:** This concerns the expression of human creativity and talent especially in visual form; also it deals with the customs, arts and social institutions of a particular group or nation.

6. **World of Business/Economy:**
This concerns the complex of human activities undertaken for profit. It concerns production and distribution. It also deals with industrial, commercial or professional operation.

7. **Social World:** This concerns the organization of and relations between people and communities.

8. **Media World:** This deals with the means of communication with large numbers of people.

Discovering your talent early in one or more of these spheres of life, nurturing, developing and engaging it is key to your leadership development, success in life and becoming influential.

2

BELIEVE YOU HAVE A TALENT

"Everybody is talented because everybody who is human has something to express."— *Brenda Ueland*

Do I really have a talent? Am I gifted? These are the questions I hear people ask on a daily basis. Even when I go to speak at conferences, people ask these questions over and over again. I bet someone reading this book is probably asking this same question too. I have good news for you. Remember earlier in this book we said that everyone has a Coin as the starting point. I do not intend to just excite you, I just want to tell you the truth and nothing but the truth. I believe that everyone has a unique set of talents and strengths. Yes, everyone has talents including you! It is important you know what they are so that you can leverage on them to add more value to your life.

Many years ago, 1998 to be precise, I saw a Bible verse I had never seen before and that marked a turn-around in my destiny. It made me discover my real self and helped me to develop focus. I discovered the leader in me and became a person of influence, it is the reason I am where I am today. I became a man on a mission. This same information is what I want to share with you, and I pray that your testimony will by far be greater than what I have experienced.

In the book of Romans Chapter 12 verse 6a (NLT) I saw these very words:

God has given to each of us the ability to do certain things well.

Please do not just read this as one of those statements. It is a fact. Whether you believe it or not, it is true. You are better off if you believe it. There are three points of emphasis in that sentence;

1. "God has given" Take note that the word "given" there is in past perfect tense. It is not that God is

going to give, He has already given.

2. "To each of us". —"Each of us" implies everyone. There is no exception. You can actually substitute the "each of us" with your name.

3. "The ability to do certain things well" -- this means that God has wired you with ability, gift or talent for doing certain things well. Take note that it is not all things well, but certain things. You can connect this with Exodus, Chapter 31 which we have considered earlier. The fact that you have not discovered this ability, gift or talent, does not mean that it does not exist. This means there is an ability you have to do something such that even when you wake you up from sleep and a demand is placed on that ability, you will deliver.

To further buttress the point that everyone is talented, Dan on leadership wrote this article in May 2012;" The NBC TV show America's Got Talent" in its 7th Season. Americas Got Talent is a contest to find the most talented people in America. It features some interesting people who

"God has given to each of us the ability to do certain things well".
Rom.14:6a

showcase their unique talents or lack of talents in hopes of winning the million dollar prize and moving on to fame. The individuals or teams who make it to the finals have found, developed, and focused on their talents. They have maximized their talents while the people who are quickly eliminated often have an unrealistic image of their true talents. This TV show can show and teach us that everyone has talents. However, not everyone has fully discovered them."

When you see the different presentations, you will be fully convinced that everyone has talents including you reading this book. There is something you can do very well better than so many people. It is just that you have not bothered to discover it.

Mark Twain also wrote a wonderful story illustrating this point in his book *"The Greatest General"*:

A man died and met Saint Peter at the gates of heaven. Recognizing the Saint's knowledge and wisdom, he wanted to ask him a question. "Saint Peter', he said, "I have been interested in military history for many years. Tell me, who was the greatest general of all times?" Peter quickly responded, "O that is a simple question. It's that man right over there."

The man looked where Peter was pointing and answered, "You must be mistaken. I knew that man on earth, and he was just a common labourer." "That's right", Peter remarked, "but he would have been the greatest general of all time if he had been a general."

This man lived and died a labourer. Probably he belonged to the class of people who feel they don't have any talent. That is why Dr. Myles Munroe said that it is at the burial grounds that you will find the greatest song writer we never had, the greatest architect we never had etc.

This then means that you and I can personalize the scripture in Romans chapter 12 verse 6 for better understanding. It will read something like this: God has given me (Uba Nd) the ability to do certain things well. Can you imagine if this truth dawns on you? Believing and accepting this fact is the beginning of a march towards success and living a life of fulfilment.

"You must believe that you have got a talent. That's the beginning of a conscious effort to discover it. That is the push you need to start the discovery journey."

If God deposited so much mineral resources thousands of feet beneath the earth worth trillions of dollars, is it possible He left man without deposits? If the birds were wired to fly, the fish to swim, then what are you wired for? There is so much deposited in every human. You must believe that you have got a talent. That's the beginning of a conscious effort to discover it. That is the push you need, to start the discovery journey. If you don't believe you have a talent, you will envy other people and may not find fulfilment in this life. If you don't believe you have a coin, you will live a 'beggars' life. If our nation can focus on educating people to understand that everyone is gifted, we are on the path to a leadership revolution.

3

HOW DO I DISCOVER MY TALENTS?

We all have a talent to offer to the world. You are the missing part of a very important puzzle of the world. The main obstacle is actually identifying your talents-
Anonymous

I was confronted with this question sometime in a class where I was teaching and without much thought about the answer, a question flashed in my mind. I suddenly gazed at the person and asked: Do you know and understand yourself? Who are you? Of course, many people can't answer these questions. We have tried to know and understand physics, chemistry and other sciences but we have never tried to learn about ourselves. We are ignorant of who we really are. Learning about yourself is one of the most important steps you will ever take towards becoming successful in life. The fact is that 90% of people on earth do not know much about themselves and are not bothered about it. You imagine people make such statements like "I never knew I could do this or that". I personally never knew I had the ability to write the book you are holding, it is amazing!

This brings out the importance of studying yourself. A wise man said, "know yourself to improve yourself". Studying yourself comprehensively will place you in *"know yourself to improve yourself"* Auguste Comte a position of avoiding failure in life and becoming a person of authority and influence.

"Why do I need to study myself?" You may ask

The Bible says in Psalm 139:14 (NLT) .*Thank you for making me so wonderfully complex! Your workmanship is marvelous, how well I know it.*

So you need to learn and study yourself because

you have a complex make up and you are wonderfully made as a proof of the workmanship of God. If you appreciate this, then the process of identifying your talent will start with an observation of yourself. That is, observing yourself to know how many things you can do unusually or exceptionally, which are your talents. To do this you need to embark on a voyage to self-discovery.

"I want to challenge you today to get out of your comfort zone. You have so much incredible potential on the inside. God has put gifts and talents in you that you probably don't know anything about. Discover them and your life is on wheels to your destiny" -**Joel Osteen**

To discover your talents will require getting into yourself and answering some key questions that will offer a clue to your gift. George Lucas hit the nail on the head when he said that "everybody has a talent; it's just a matter of moving around until you have discovered what it is." Also note that it is never too late to discover your talent. You may have to take a sheet of paper and a pen to a quiet environment and answer the following questions.

"everybody has a talent; it's just a matter of moving around until you have discovered what it is."
George Lucas

WHAT DO YOU ENJOY OR LOVE DOING THE MOST?

This is a very important lead to your gift. The fact that you enjoy indulging in that activity is a clue to the way you are wired. The word "most" here means that you love or enjoy doing many things but there is one that stands out, which has something to do with your talent. You may not consider them as gifts or talents, but if you enjoy them that much, chances are that there is something there that can lead you to your gifts. You must also ask yourself a basic question; "What is that thing that whenever am doing it I lose track of time". Whatever it is, has a connection with

"I want to challenge you today to get out of your comfort zone. You have so much incredible potential on the inside. God has put gifts and talents in you that you probably don't

something in your inside. These are things that you don't need anyone to remind you or compel you to do. I enjoy public speaking to the extent that whenever am talking to a group of people, I don't want to stop. I don't even mind paying them to sit down and listen to me. Anything you don't mind paying so much for people to allow you do, is your talent.

WHAT DID YOU ALWAYS DREAM ABOUT

DOING OR
BECOMING AS A KID?

What you have always dreamt about becoming or doing as a kid is a pointer to your gift. Flash back to what used to catch your interest as a kid. Remember those simple things that made you incredibly happy as a child. Our hidden talents are often buried in our past, but have not resurfaced in our adult life.

"Anything you do not mind paying so much for people to allow you do is your talent."

Keep a story journal to trigger your memory of the times you felt happiest and start to infuse those instances into your present life. You may discover, or re-discover your hidden talents. An example is Wilbur and Orville, the Wright brothers who were credited with building and flying the first heavier-than-air powered aircraft. They achieved the first recorded flight on 17th December 1903 and over the next 10 years, they continued to develop the aircraft making a significant contribution to the development of the modern airplane.

"Our hidden talents are often buried in our past, but have not resurfaced in our adult life."

How did this come about? In 1878, when Orville and Wilbur were aged 7 and 11 respectively, their father brought them a toy "helicopter." It was based on an invention by French aeronautical pioneer Alphonse Penaud. Made of cork, bamboo, and paper, with a rubber band to twirl its twin blades, it was a little bigger than an adult's hand. They later said this sparked their interest in flight and led to their discovering their gift in mechanical engineering with a bias in aeronautics. A word for parents, one of the best things you can do for your children is to help them discover their talents early in life and help them choose courses that place a demand on those talents and watch that child become great in life. This comes from a close observation of our children and watch for recurring patterns in their behaviour.

WHAT IS THE ONE THING YOU DO EFFORTLESSLY?

Whatever you didn't go to school to learn or acquire in any training yet you repeatedly do it with relative ease without struggle to the extent that people marvel is your talent. It comes natural and easy for you. As you are reading this book, pause and ask yourself, what are the things I do without struggle such that even if someone should

"A word for parents, one of the best things you can do for your children is to help them discover their talents early in life and help them choose courses that place a demand on those talents and watch that child become great in life."

29

wake me from sleep, I will still do it with ease. If you continually struggle at anything, it may not be your talent. From my youth, I discovered that I can organize activities with ease. People marvel at my ability to do this. The fact that I didn't acquire it made me understand that I was born with it. It's my gift.

STEP OUT OF YOUR COMFORT ZONE
Many people fail to discover their talents because they fear to try anything new, they fear to take risks and they prefer to live in their comfort zones. Once you start going out of your comfort zone, you will find out about your real talents. Some people are scared of handling positions of leadership without knowing that they may have a leadership gift. Overcoming that fear might just be what will unlock that gift in them.

WHAT ARE YOU PASSIONATE ABOUT?
Your talents are hidden in your passion. Passion is a strong feeling of enthusiasm or excitement for something or about doing something. This strong feeling comes from within and not from outside. Your passion is what drives you to that section of the newspaper or magazine each time you pick one. Be it sports, health, religion, politics, travel, movies, fashion etc. Those things you have passion for are

clues to your gift.

ASK YOUR FAMILY

FAMILY here is an acronym. An excellent way to identify your talents is to ask people who have known you over a long time the things they think you are good at. Most times they notice things about you which you tend to neglect.

F----FAMILY

A----ASSOCIATES (FRIENDS)

M---MINISTRY (CHURCH)

I----INSPIRATOR (MENTOR)

L----LEARNING (CLASS MATES)

Y---YOURSELF

Listen carefully to what they have to say. They must have noticed some common traits you have exhibited over time. This is a very important way of identifying your talents.

TURN TO GOD

God is the author of talents. He is our creator. He put those abilities in us. By the Holy Spirit He fashioned us. Pray to God and ask Him to reveal your talents to you. He assured us that if we pray, He will answer us.

Jeremiah 33:3

Call unto me, and I will answer thee, and show thee great and mighty things, which thou knowest not. (KJV)

These are few exercises you can try out to help you discover your talents. Recognize that you can have more than one gift, but there is always one that is more predominant than the rest, which is the one you should pay most attention to. Also some gifts complement one another. My emphasis in all these comes from the point that every manufacturer knows the strengths and the weaknesses of his product. Our manufacturer is God and He gave us our talents. This means that His guidance is key to discovering them.

"Our manufacturer is God and He gave us our talents. This means that His guidance is key to discovering them."

4

HOW TO DEVELOP YOUR TALENT

A winner is somebody who recognizes his God-given talents, works his tail off to develop them into skills and uses these skills to accomplish his goals. –Larry Bird.

We have established that everyone has a coin. That is to say that everyone has a gift/talent. The fact is that the talent you possess right now is like potential energy or stored energy. It has a potential to do so many things, but needs an external force to act on it to become effective. It needs to change to kinetic energy

(energy in motion) for it to profit you. The coin you possess cannot do much for you except you do business with it. If you spend it, it's gone. But you can multiply the coin by investing it. This is the same with your talent, it is at its raw state. You need to move that talent from its raw state into a finished product that can attract attention. You need to invest in your talent, and nurture it to prominence.

Pope John II said

"Artistic talent is a gift from God and whoever discovers it in himself has a certain obligation: to know that he cannot waste this talent but must develop it"

It was Ralph Wald O. Emerson that said "Every artist was first an amateur".

This is a profound statement. Nobody was born a superstar. Every success story was first no story; every great talent we celebrate today was first raw. Nobody was ever born a finished product. Every billionaire you see today first started with a

"Artistic talent is a gift from God and whoever discovers it in himself has a certain obligation: to know that he cannot waste this talent but must develop it"
Pope John Paul II

coin, but they were willing to invest that coin for it to multiply. It is important you develop that talent you possess. It is the process for your being handed a staff.

Developing your talent requires a lot of drive and effort just like developing any career. Some talents require less drive and effort to develop than others. Example, the effort required to develop your talent as a doctor will be more than that required to develop your talent as a driver, so do not be discouraged if someone develops his faster than you are doing. The following factors are going to help you in growing and nurturing your talent.

"Every artist was first an amateur"
Ralph W. Emerson

BELIEVE IN YOURSELF
"The strongest factor for success is self-esteem: Believing you can do it, believing you deserve it, believing you will get it"-Anonymous

The first step to developing your talent is believing in your ability to do so. You are an extraordinary creation with unlimited abilities deposited in you. You must have faith in yourself. Every product serves a purpose, and the manufacturer wires the product with the abilities inside to fulfil that purpose. A fan has the ability to rotate and circulate air when turned on. God who is our manufacturer has put in you the necessary requirements to proceed and develop your talent. The Bible says in *Philippians 2: 13 (KJV)*

–For it is God which worketh in you both to will and to do of his good pleasure.

You can develop that gift and become the best in your generation. That's why Bible says that

"I can do all things through Christ that strengthens me". Philippians 4: 13.

Just like Stephanie Lahart said in her book "Overcoming Life obstacles: Enlighten - Encourage - Empower", "No longer will I doubt my abilities...I will give myself a chance.

That should be your confession.

"Never you say "I cannot". Delete it from your vocabulary. God says you can develop your talent. If you do not believe, you will hinder God from

"No longer will I doubt my abilities...I will give myself a chance."

Stephanie Lahart

manifesting greatly in you.

He also said *that all things are possible to him that believes. Mark 9:23 (KJV).*

When you believe, you will see the Glory of God in your talent. Just as it is written in John 11:40 (KJV).

"Jesus saith unto her, Said I not unto thee, that, if thou wouldest believe, thou shouldest see the glory of God?"

This is the beginning of you becoming a person of influence and authority which is symbolic of the Staff.

Also there is something you have to consciously do, that is to be fully convinced about the talent you have. Have a serious conviction that your talent is a goldmine; appreciate it as something unique and precious. See it as a deposit of God inside you. The

"You can never get to your full potential in life if you lack faith in both yourself and your talent"

lack of conviction is the reason some people discover their talents and it ends there. There is no consciousness to do anything about their talent. Your talent has the potential to put a staff of leadership and authority in your hands. Failure to believe in your talent will keep you in the dark and in obscurity. You can never get to your full potential in life if you lack faith in both yourself and your talent. In fact this book in your hands would have reached you many years ago if I had believed in my ability to write. But when I said "I can" and "I believe" that transformed into the precious gift you have in your hands, this can be your story too. Change your mentality and believe in yourself and in your abilities.

YOU NEED TO HAVE VISION

Dream lofty dreams, and as you dream, so shall you become. Your vision is the promise of what you shall one day be. Your ideal is the prophecy of what you shall at last unveil -James Allen

A vision is something that you can imagine or a picture that you see in your mind about the future. You have a coin in your hand. For that to multiply, you must imagine or see it explode to millions. It is called a perception of the future. Your talent is a raw material you have that has

"Dream lofty dreams, and as you dream, so shall you become. Your vision is the promise of what you shall one day be. Your ideal is the prophecy of what you shall at last unveil".
James Allen

to be transformed to a finished product that can be marketed worldwide. It should become a global phenomenon. For that to happen, you must first see it with your eyes of faith. You must be able to write down and vividly describe what you see concerning your talent and where it can take you because it has the potential to lift you from obscurity to limelight.

That's why the Bible says in *Habakkuk 2:2;*

And the Lord answered me, and said, write the vision, and make it plain upon tables, that he run that readeth it. (KJV).

What you see about your talent, and write down, with hardwork, is what it will become. The big question is, in twenty years where will you be with your talent? This is a serious food for thought. If you are a talented lawyer, see yourself as becoming the best senior advocate of Nigeria (SAN).The Bible also says

Where there is no vision the people cast off restraint. Proverbs 29:18.NKJV.
This means that when you do not work with a vision in mind, you will live a careless life and not be focused. You will find yourself tolerating anything, with no consciousness of excellence. Your conscious awareness of your vision ignites your passion. That is

why a wise man said that: "If there is nothing that makes you jump out of your bed early in the morning, sleeping becomes very interesting."

Build a vision around that talent and watch it develop wings and fly.

Equally T. E. Lawrence in his book "Seven Pillars of Wisdom" said: "All men dream but not equally. Those who dream by night in the dusty recesses of their minds wake in the day to find it was vanity but the dreamers of the day are dangerous men, for they may act their dream with open eyes to make it possible." When I talk about dreams and visions, it is not the night visions by fake prophets or dreams resulting from over feeding in the night. I am talking about a conscious effort to imagine your future. The staff is awaiting men and women who are ready to grasp and hold a vision. It is the very essence of successful leadership. The direct result of living a vision is influence and authority.

"If there is nothing that makes you jump out of your bed early in the morning, sleeping becomes very interesting."
Anonymous

"Pursue knowledge as though it is your life blood, then you will know greatness!"
Monique Rockliffe.

GO FOR KNOWLEDGE, UNDERSTANDING & WISDOM

We are no longer in the dispensation of age and experience. We are in the era of knowledge and information. Information leads a true leader and a true leader leads others –Israel Ayivor

A coin will remain a coin if you do not do something or trade with it. Trading with it, will require information- What kind of business to do, understanding how to do it, where to do it. All these are products of information. Without understanding, right knowledge and wisdom you will fail in anything you are doing. Albert Einsten observed, *"Any fool can know, the point is to understand"*.

The very next step to developing your talent is to go for knowledge and have understanding of your talent. Look for a way to learn about your talent and do all you can to be the best. The absence of knowledge and understanding in any field of endeavour is the presence of mediocrity. Go for every information you can get in that field. If you are talented as an architect, you must read books by Frank Lloyd Wright and Le

"Any fool can know, the point is to understand"
– Albert Einsten.

Cembuser etc. If you are talented in leadership, you must read materials written by men like Dr. Myles Munroe, John C. Maxwell, Brain Tracy etc. Search for great authors who have excelled in the same area of talent you have and seek to read their articles. I am gifted in leadership. I have a library of over a hundred books and have searched the internet severally to update my knowledge of leadership. I have prayed to God for understanding and wisdom in pursuit of developing this talent of mine. I always remind God what He said in the Bible:

If any of you lack wisdom, let him ask of God, that giveth to all men liberally, and upbraideth not; and it shall be given him. (James 1:5 KJV)

You can pause and join me and ask Him for wisdom in case you lack it, for He said "it shall be given to you"

By the grace of God, I have come to a certain point of relevance in my society. My passion to develop my talent has brought me to a point where I am influencing a lot of people. I speak with authority when it comes to the subject of leadership. The staff has been delivered to my hands which is a symbol of influence and authority which speaks of leadership. Remember God said in Hosea 4:6a (KJV)

My people are destroyed for lack of knowledge…

The great scientist Albert Einstein was asked the secret of his success, he replied;
I merely stand on the shoulders of men who have gone ahead of me.

This means his ability to leverage on the knowledge of great men who have excelled before.

Talent without knowledge and understanding will amount to nothing. Knowledge is power. The last four letters in knowledge is edge. When you have knowledge it gives you an edge over others who do not. Sources of this knowledge may include: books, movies, lessons, songs, family members and friends. Note that it is important to seek for right knowledge.
Do not just in the quest for knowledge read anything. Certain information could have negative effects on you, seek for books, movies etc. recommended by your mentors, pastors and role models.

Application of this knowledge is critical to your developing your talent. Knowledge without application is simply a waste. Applying the knowledge to one's life is wisdom and the Bible says that wisdom is profitable to direct.

Wisdom is the principal thing: therefore get wisdom: and with all thy getting get understanding. Proverbs 4:7

GET RELEVANT SKILLS
Another important way to develop your gift is to add relevant skills to your talent. Skill can be defined as the ability and capacity acquired through training and experience (deliberate systematic and sustained effort) to smoothly and adaptively carry out complex activities. You can be very talented but lack of relevant skill to enhance that talent can mess you up. Imagine a very talented music artist who doesn't have good stage management skill, does not know how to hold the microphone, or how to transpose and does not have good stage carriage. These are some relevant skills that can enhance the talent of singing. The person in question here can only pass for a local champion who cannot get to *"Every talent requires a skill for success"* the top of his or her career. If you are a talented teacher or an orator, you need effective skills in public speaking. These skills most times are developed from trainings and seminars. So you have to first identify those skills relevant to your gift, and seek out seminars/trainings and workshops

where you can acquire them. You must be ready to spend money to attend these programs. Note that every talent requires a skill for success.

PASSION/DESIRE–

Find out what makes you come alive. Whatever it is, become it and let it become you, and great things happen for you, to you and because of you-Anonymous

For you to develop and grow the coin in your hands, there must be a passion to do this. The desire must be there. Mike Murdock says that the evidence of desire is pursuit. Your passion is the life and energy of your talent. That is what would

"When you fuel your passion and fan aflame your desire, your talent will grow."

ensure that you do not quit because there will be obstacles. When you fuel your passion and fan aflame your desire, your talent will grow. It is this passion that will make you grab every opportunity to display your talent. It will also get you to read all you can lay your hands on, listen to every message and watch every movie that has to do with your talent.

Neglecting passion blocks creative flow. When you are passionate, you are energized. Likewise, when you lack passion, your energy is low and unproductive. Energy is everything when it comes to being successful.

HARD WORK/PRACTICE

... Work hard and become a leader, be lazy and become a slave
Proverbs 12:24 (NLT).

It takes hard work to be successful in business. You have a coin in your hands and for it to multiply and increase, hard work is needed. I know you have heard it a thousand times before, but it is true that hard work pays off. For your talent to be developed, you need hard work. Growth in anything never comes cheap. If you want to be good at anything, you have to practise, practise and practise.

Larry Bird, the legendary basketball player who is one of the best all time players with career highlights as 3 times NBA Champion, 2 times NBA finals MVP, 3 times NBA most valuable players award etc. became a legend because of his work ethic. He was not the quickest or the strongest but he discovered his talent early

"There is no substitute for hard work".
Thomas Edison

"The artist is nothing without the gift, the gift is nothing without work".
Emile Zola

in life, and started developing it . His competitiveness and desire to become better was second to none. His daily program for so many years included a long-distance run, practice games with team mates, multiple sit-ups and short-distance runs all sandwiched between lengthy shooting drills. In fact, it was said that he practised about 500 free throws every morning, no wonder he became one of the best in history in shooting free throws and scoring 3 points. He sums up the effect of hard work by saying:

"I have got a theory that if you give 100% all of the time, somehow things will work out in the end."No wonder Thomas Edison said that "There is no substitute for hard work".

Also note that there are many highly talented people, but what separates the talented person from the successful one is a lot of hard work. Success does not so much depend on your abilities as much as your choices.   Any lack of skill can be more than made up by how hard you work toward a goal you care about.

In the words of Emile Zola, "The artist is nothing without the gift, the gift is nothing without work".

Bible summarizes by saying in Proverbs 22:9

Seest thou a man diligent in his business? He shall stand before kings; he shall not stand before mean men.

I learnt early in life that one of the gift I have is the ability to organize events. Have worked hard at this and it has become noticeable to many. Little wonder when Dr. Myles Munroe visited Imo State, I was one of the few called to organize his visit and the programmes he came for. I had the privilege of being foremost in the crew that received him at the airport and we were driven in a convoy to the government house where we were received by the governor of Imo State.

Hard work in the area of your talent will take you to the palace and place you side by side with great people. Though your beginning might have been small, your latter end will greatly increase as you work hard. Add hard work to developing your talent and you are on your way to becoming influential.

"you don't enter the ring to become a champion rather you become in your training and enter the ring to be announced as the champion".

It is said that practise makes perfect. The more you practise your talent, the better you become. As a musician, the more you spend long hours rehearsing, the more you overcome your weaknesses. Mike Murdock said "you don't enter the ring to become a champion, rather you become a champion in your training/practise only to enter the ring to be announced as the champion.

The Staff is awaiting you.

YOU NEED TO LEARN FROM THE EXPERTS (A COACH OR A MENTOR)

One of the great keys to success is to use proven success methods learnt from the experts, don't try to re-invent the wheel. Life is too short – Brian Tracy.

There are experts in every area of talent. If you desire to grow your talent, discover someone who has excelled in that area and learn the principles he practised and you will become successful. Every talent is grown on the training ground, and every training ground is manned by a coach. This can be buttressed citing the field of sports where athletes engage the services of someone who has had an outstanding carrier to guide them to greatness. Whether you are talented as a doctor, engineer, architect, sportsman etc. you need to learn under someone who can guide you because most outstanding and successful people had mentors.

A mentor is someone who serves as a trusted counsellor or teacher, especially in occupational setting. In the words of Tom Landry, "a coach is someone who tells you what you don't want to hear, who has you see what you don't want to see, so you could be who you have always known you could be". This is perfect, in a bid to develop your talent, we need to be guided by people who have obtained results worthy of emulation, so that we can imitate them and get better results. This is because the joy of every mentor (coach) is to produce someone greater than himself/herself.

The little success I have recorded in life in the area of my talent (Leadership) is because I have a mentor/coach – Festus Azarah. I met him for the first time in 1996 and there was a connection. I

"No man is capable of self-improvement if he sees no other model but himself."
Corvado I. Genaroso

did not know anything about leadership, but he saw the talent in me when I didn't even notice it and started grooming and coaching me. A mentor helps you discover rich purposes and abilities in you. He bought me the first ever leadership book I read (*21 most powerful minutes in a leaders day*– John C. Maxwell) and the rest is now history. I followed hard after him though it wasn't easy. He was hard on me, instilling the discipline and the character required to develop my talent. He is a great leader with results. I started by copying the principles he practised and started posting results too. He thought me and prevailed on me to become a reader. I knew he had something I was looking for.

Corvado I. Genaroso said – no man is capable of self - improvement if he sees no other model but himself.

To receive the staff of authority in the area of your talent, you need to stand on the shoulders of men who have gone ahead of you.

A mentor will offer direction and useful advice having passed through obstacles in the area in question. He ensures that his student doesn't fail in his task.

A word of advice here, for you to get a mentor, get one in the area of your talent. Make sure he is very successful and has a good character worthy of emulation. Find out if he is willing to be transparent with you, be transparent too and give him every information about yourself he needs to assist you with and learn as much as possible from him.

LEARN TO SET GOALS

Setting goals is the first step in turning the invisible into the visible - Tony Robins

It has been found that the ability to effectively set goals throughout life is one of the most important skills that any of us can have. It is a factor that can help and motivate you towards developing your talent. Goal setting in broad terms is the process of deciding on something you want, planning how to get it, and then working towards the objective. This is the ability to take a large activity (such as your dream) and break it down into smaller more manageable parts (goals). This presents a more realistic approach to accomplishing the big task. Everyone must be able to set goals.

On a personal level, setting goals is a process that allows people to specify their objectives then work towards these

"Goal setting is the strongest human force for motivation."
Paul Meyer

objectives. This means that after writing down your vision for your talent which is your destination, the next thing is to set weekly, monthly and yearly goals which are a break down into smaller units of that vision you have. These goals will include the necessary skills to acquire the knowledge you need to have, and certain habits to develop.

Goal setting is not wishing or dreaming. It is something that is progressively worked towards. You must decide what you want to accomplish with your talent and start setting goals to accomplish it.
Paul Meyer *said* that "Goal setting is the strongest human force for motivation."

Taking note of the following characteristics of goals will help you set goals effectively so you can develop your talent and achieve positive results in your career.

1. Define your goals with clarity.

The goal should be very specific. Be precise in what you want. The more clearly defined your goal is, the easier it will be to attain. For example if you believe that you are talented as a doctor, what branch of medicine is your talent best suited? Where do you want to *"You must constantly push yourself to move outside your "comfort zone".* end up? Is it as a consultant or a professor? As you can see, there are many questions to ask and the more questions you ask yourself and are able to answer, the clearer your goal will be. Once you know the exact outcome you want, you will be able to create an action plan that will ensure you develop your talent.

These are decisions you must make and you have to be specific. Remember, it is specialization in your talent that enhances your worth in the society and not as a general practitioner. You have heard the phrase "jack of all trade but master of none". These are people who feel they are good at everything but can never amount to anything in one. Ability to determine exactly what it is you want to accomplish with your talent will motivate you into action to develop your talent.

2. Make your goals inspirational

You need to set goals grand enough to challenge yourself. Example, in the year 2002, I set a 5-year goal for myself to become one of the best Youth Conference speakers and leadership trainers in Imo State.

"If you do not have a date on it, the goal is only a wish or a dream."

This required developing my talent to a point of relevance in the society. For me, I was nowhere near that by the year 2002. It was challenging and demanding for me. Remember that if you do not push yourself beyond your current limits to reach your goals, then you are not really achieving anything. To develop your talent and be truly successful and reach your true potential, you must constantly push yourself to move outside your "comfort zone".

3. Write your goals down.
Don't just think it, ink it-Anonymous

Always jot down your goals. This is powerful. The process of physically seeing your goals helps crystallize them in your mind. This process also better enables you to be committed to them. This means that when you set goals on how to develop your talent and you jot them down, physically seeing that goal does something to your mind and converges your whole energy towards that goal. I have practised it and it works. You experience a surge and drive from within towards attaining your goal. You have to buy a notebook and write down your goals consciously because the faintest line is thicker than the thickest memory.

Interesting fact: A popular Harvard Business School study once found that only 3% of the population record their goals in writing. Another 14% have goals but do not write them down, whereas 83% do not even have clearly defined goals. More interesting is that this 3% earned an astounding ten times that of the 83% group!

4. Determine deadline for accomplishing your

goal.

Crystallize your goals. Make a plan for achieving them and set yourself a deadline. Then, with supreme confidence, determination and disregard for obstacles and other people's criticisms, carry out your plan. -Paul J. Meyer

A goal must be time definitive. For you to be motivated towards daily developing your talent, your goal must have a deadline. If you do not have a date on it, the goal is only a wish or a dream. If you set a goal for instance "I will read books written by great men who have excelled in my area of talent". This is without any deadline, you might as well accomplish it in the next 5 years. But such a goal should read something like this "I will finish a book every week written by great men who have excelled in my area of talent". Now this is a goal. That deadline is a check on you, whenever you read that goal you are challenged to do something before every week runs out.

"Set small goals and build upon them".
Lee Haney

5. Make sure the goal is believable to you
Make sure the goals you set are realistic and realizable. If you believe they are impossible or

ambiguous to achieve, you will never take the necessary action required. It will deflate your confidence and drive. Imagine a lawyer who just graduated from the university setting a goal to be the best lawyer in Nigeria in 6 months. That is a night dream. Lee Haney put it this way, "Exercise to stimulate, not to annihilate. The world wasn't formed in a day, and neither were we. Set small goals and build upon them". These characteristics will help you formulate a clear and accurate goal statement for accomplishing the goal of developing your talent. A good way to remember how a goal statement should be defined is the old S.M.A.R.T acronym used by many experts in goal setting. S.M.A.R.T stands for:

S—Specific
M—Measurable
A—Action oriented
R—Realistic
T—Time and resource constrained.

Also note the following;

Where are you now?
Take a current inventory of where you are now in developing your talent. This will help in setting your goals because you will never know how far you have to go if you don't know where you already are.

What obstacles do you need to overcome?
Are there some things that may make it difficult for you to achieve your goal? Be aware of the obstacles so you can make plans to overcome them.

What knowledge will you need to acquire?
Will you need to take certain courses or attend certain trainings to enhance your talent? Will you need research into new markets?

What organizations and groups should you associate with?
Are there certain groups of people that can make it easier for you to accomplish the goal of developing your talent? Remember your network determines your net worth.

What are the benefits to you?
Write down as many benefits as possible that will accrue to you as you develop your talent. The more the benefits you can come up with, the more likely you will be to stick to the goal until it is achieved.

Develop an action plan
Determine the steps that will be necessary to achieve your goal. Start from the accomplishment of the goal and work backwards.

Take daily action towards your goal.
The dream you have for your talents and your goals to develop yourself will require action. The greatest goal in the world will never materialize unless consistent action is taken.

Resolve never to quit.
Decide that you will never give up, even when times are tough, until your goal is reached.

Frequent review and re-assessment.
Goal setting is definitely an ongoing process that is accomplished over time. When we first sit down and start to define goals it can seem like a difficult and daunting task but over time, it begins to get much easier. Patience is required.

All goals due the following year should be reviewed at least once a week and daily if possible. The great thing about frequent review is that this forces us to make big decisions and determine priorities in our life. We should keep watch over goals that are not being achieved on time or for goals on which we keep

"Procrastination is the bad habit of putting off until the day after tomorrow what should have been done the day

extending the deadline.

Don't procrastinate.

Procrastination is opportunity's assassin

Procrastination is the bad habit of putting off until the day after tomorrow what should have been done the day before yesterday. It is a dream killer. Understand that the only way to achieve goals is to take action! Knowledge means nothing if you don't apply it.

5

IMPORTANCE OF TALENT

TALENT- A TOOL FOR EVANGELISM

You are the light of the world – like a city on a mountain, glowing in the night for all to see. Don't put your light under a basket! Instead, put it on a stand for all. In the same way, let your good deeds shine out for all to see, so that everyone can praise your heavenly father. (Mt 5:14 – 16 NLT).

I believe strongly that our talents and gifts are vital for spreading the good news of our Lord Jesus and His salvation. This is one area the church has not paid attention to. When you excel in your talent, it attracts a lot of attention, widens your sphere of influence and lots of people begin to see you as a role model and mentor. At this point they are willing to know how you were able to get to the top and follow the same path. This is where evangelism comes in for us Christians, we point them to our Lord Jesus Christ and our new life in Christ as the reason for our excellence in our talents.

When we develop our talents to a point of prominence, we become like a city on a mountain like the Bible says. We begin to shine there for the world to see, whether in the field of Sports, Academics, Politics, Business, and Entertainment etc. People cannot wait to hear us. This is why we ought to strive to become the best there is in our talents. An example can be seen at the 2007 FIFA World Cup co-hosted by South Korea and Japan. Brazil won the World Cup as they exhibited excellence by showcasing ingenious football talents. It was recorded that over 2.5 billion people were watching the finals live. Most of the Brazilians wore inner T-shirts with the inscription "Jesus is
Lord". When the game was over they lifted their Jerseys and the whole world was reading their T-shirts. They preached a message to over 2.5 billion

people at once which no preacher or evangelist has ever done till date.

The Bible says in *Deuteronomy 28:13 KJV-And the Lord shall make you the head, and not the tail.*

It makes a lot of impact preaching the gospel as the head. We Christians have paid less attention to the subject of talent, while unbelievers have taken it seriously and are influencing a lot of our youths negatively with it. We need to wake up.

"The talents and abilities we have inside us have the potential to become billions of dollars."

Another example is the FIFA World Best Footballer for 2007, Kaka, an Evangelical practising Christian who while receiving his award in a live televised program attributed his success to God. After every goal, Kaka raises his eyes and hands to thank God, and he thanks God for his talents. Perhaps his most famous statements was when his team, AC Milan, won a championship game and Kaka tore off his soccer jersey to reveal a T-shirt that read " I belong to Jesus". He could not have been more eloquent than that and as an evangelical Christian, he feels the need to convert non-followers. He once said!

"To those who already have Jesus, you have the best choice and are in the best team. Go ahead. Do not give up. The fight is great, but we can only win being on Jesus' side. To those who have not yet surrendered their lives to Jesus; what are you doing being outside of this team? Come to learn the word of God, come to know who God really is!"

Through his talent, he has won countless souls for the Lord as a result of reaching the pinnacle of his career. My wife is a Senior Optometrist with the Health Management Board, Imo State. She is talented as an Optometrist and very passionate about her profession. By excelling in her talent, she has affected so many people and counselled them in the ways of the Lord. There are many people who have excelled in their talents; they are using them as major tools to bring many people to Christ.

The truth is that the higher you climb in life the more influential you become and the more eyes are on you.

TALENT – YOUR MAJOR SOURCE OF WEALTH

...But remember your Lord your God, for it is He who gives you the ... ability to produce wealth, and so confirms His covenant, which He swore to your

ancestors, as it is today (Deuteronomy 8 : 18 NIV)

Everything in life is a product of gift, and every person is a storehouse of talents. God has given us these innate abilities for our profiting. The talents and abilities we have inside us have the potential to become billions of dollars. Examples include the minerals we have thousands of feet below the earth like gold, diamond, crude oil etc. As long as they are undiscovered and undeveloped, they are useless to any nation. But when they are discovered, mined and refined, they become such huge resources that can sustain continents financially. In fact, I cannot quantify in dollars what they have been worth over the years. The talents you are born with are like that. As long as you do not go thousands of feet inside you to discover, mine and refine them, poverty will be staring at you. Those talents are potential wealth stored up in you. Investing in your talent is a worthy investment.

FROM TALENT TO WEALTH

Successful people have agreed that there are some basic principles that govern turning your talent into wealth. These principles are generally accepted truth that work anywhere in the world. They do not depend on where

"Unless you can do a particular thing in a way beyond what an average person can do, it might not generate you income".

you come from, where you are, your height, age, or colour. They do not discriminate. Once you can apply the basic truth it will work for you and the good news about it is that they can be learnt by anyone including you.

Development of your identified talent is the key to turning your talent into wealth. This is because an underdeveloped talent or potential will never lead to wealth.

In an article "Turning your Talent to Wealth" from the internet by Hub pages it was said that "Developing one's abilities in this regard means bringing them to such a standard at which they are above the competence of an average person, speaking in this connection, unless you can do a particular thing in a way beyond what an average person can do, it might not generate you income".

"Premature satisfaction with half-success is a

This is perfect, Mike Murdock puts it this way, "give someone what he cannot get elsewhere and he will keep coming to you". Money is an exchange for service. You must be able to serve your talent above what the average person can do to be able to attract people to part with money for that service.

For example, as an architect, doctor, singer etc., you must be able to develop that talent to a point where your delivery is better than what your peers can offer, if not people will not look for you. If you are displaying your talent the same way others are doing theirs, you will get the same result they are getting. Furthermore the same online article continues:

"Development also involves ability to withstand social criticism against a particular venture e.g. there was a time music as a profession was scorned as being only good for social misfits in the society but today the reverse is the case. When your abilities are developing to the point of attracting attention, you should endeavour

"If you aim at average mark you will probably remain average in life but if you aim for the sky, your thought will always be on achieving great things and you will not settle for less".

to showcase these abilities at every opportunity; do not ever expect to start off as a high income professional; few ever do. Be content with beginning as an amateur. Income should not be your priority, as you ought to concentrate your efforts on fine tuning your abilities and getting people to know your capabilities. To short-circuit means to have false sense of having "arrived" when in fact, the potential is just unfolding. Many talented persons get derailed just as their talents begin to shine. This is often caused by young talents allowing their unexpected success to get into their heads thereby losing focus of their ultimate objectives of developing their potential of becoming established professionals. Young men and women should always strive for excellence. If you aim at average mark you will probably remain average in life but if you aim for the sky, your thought will always be on achieving great things and you will not settle for less.

"A young talent with versatile knowledge in different areas has a definite edge over another fellow of similar ability that is bereft of knowledge".

Premature satisfaction with half-success is a dream-killer, nobody should indulge in it. This means you must not only invest in developing your talents, but also invest the proceeds of your abilities to make you financially stable. Imagine for instance, a young musician or artist who employs the proceeds of his amateurish performance to acquire a luxury car when he is yet to acquire musical instrument or painting equipment. Such a person may find it difficult to realize his potential. In this connection, unwise use of resources in the early part of one's career can make a year's journey to consume 10 years.

A young talent with versatile knowledge in different areas has a definite edge over another fellow of similar ability that is bereft of knowledge. Dead ends are paths of self-destruction. History is replete with cases of budding stars that killed off their dreams by engaging in activities such as injection of hard drugs, boozing, betting and other activities perilous to dream actualization. The first work of many musicians and artistes of repute had in most cases, once been adjudged unmeritorious and unmarketable and turned down by their respective recording/publishing companies. The fact that many of them turned into legends speaks volumes about the fact that there is no finality to failure.

"Failure simply means, you need to try harder to succeed, and bringing one's talent to a level where it

Failure simply means, you need to try harder to succeed, and bringing one's talent to a level where it brings in money often requires resilience, courage and self-belief. You should try to give yourself a distinct identity by inventing your own way of doing things. Even if there are ways others can do that particular thing better, doing your own in a particular way will be your own personal symbol. Do not be contented with copying others; carve a niche for yourself by being an ambassador of your own enterprise.

Finally, the importance of good character, cultivation of virtues like honesty, trustworthiness and reputation for hard work remain sine qua non for success. No matter how good a person may be at doing a thing, if he fails to keep up pace with modern trends, his skill may become irrelevant. A person should be ready to imbibe all the positive changes dictated by science and technology in his area of specialization. If you devote yourself to all these and put your trust in your God, you will be able to turn talents into profits.

"Do not be contented with copying others; carve a niche for yourself by being an ambassador of your own enterprise".

6

THE GOD FACTOR
THE AUTHOR OF TALENTS

Every good gift and perfect gift is from above, coming down from the father of lights with whom there is no variation or shadow due to change.(James 1:17 Esv)

Every good gift and perfect gift is from God. He is the author and finisher of our talents. Every talent possessed by any man was given to him by God. Remember this talent is innate, meaning you were born with it. It is a natural endowment, you did not acquire nor purchase it. Knowing this, you cannot neglect Him and do whatever you like with it. You must acknowledge Him every step with your talent for it to bring you fulfilment.

Rev. Wildfire in his article on how to develop your talent said "To ignore your talent is to ignore God in your life. To attempt to succeed apart from your talent is to insult the wisdom of God. He made things that way, just fall in line."

This is a wakeup call to many in the corporate world and some pastors who are talented in lots of areas and were serving with their talents but because of the pursuit of money or the call of God, got lucrative jobs and have neglected their talents. Nothing says that you cannot merge the two. Also there are pastors who because of the call to become pastors, have completely neglected the talents they were developing and are virtually idle in church, waiting for time to preach. It is important you get back to your talent because it is your pathway to leadership.

Acknowledging God in your life is a very important factor for you to excel in your talent. Every product manufactured has a manual of operation. You are a product of God, and in His operations manual which is the Bible,

God said in Romans 12:6a *"God has given each of us the ability to do certain things well" (NLT)*

The word "ability" is same as talent/gift as can be seen in other versions like in NIV, the same scripture reads

"In His grace, God has given us different gifts for doing certain things well".

My emphasis here is on certain things. What are these certain things? This is for your own discovery as we treated earlier.

"To ignore your talent is to ignore God in your life"
Rev. Wildfire

A child is born and suddenly at age 3 people begin to exclaim; what a wonderful voice this girl has! She did not learn the voice, or acquire it. God put it there. The same way a cousin of mine at age 3 started playing with electronic gadgets at home and everybody was amazed at his ability. God gave it to him, he did not go to any school to acquire that. Ben Carson, (one of the best neurosurgeons in the world) in his book, "Think Big" describes how at a tender age he had gifted hands with the ability to handle tiny things which led to his studying medicine with a bias in neurosurgery an area that deals with tiny brain cells. That ability was given to him by God.

TALENT AND PURPOSE
"To everything there is a season, a time for every

purpose under heaven". Ecclesiastics 3:1 KJV.

God clearly said it in His Word that everything He has created has a purpose. The gift/talent you have was given to you by God for a purpose. Dr Myles Munroe defined purpose as the original intent of a thing. There was an intent God had for giving you that talent. In his book "In the pursuit of purpose", Dr Myles Munroe said

"You must realize that fulfilment in life is dependent on your becoming and doing what you were born to be and do. For without purpose, life has no heart".
Dr. Myles Munroe

"You must realize that fulfilment in life is dependent on your becoming and doing what you were born to be and do. For without purpose, life has no heart". And I add, that what you were born to be and do is directly related to your God-given talent. For you to accomplish your mission here on earth, you will need your talents.

Dr Myles Munroe also said, when you want to know the purpose of a thing, you don't ask the thing or any other but the manufacturer. God has the answer to what your purpose is. That is why in Jeremiah 33:3; He said

"Call unto me, and I will answer thee, and shew thee great and mighty things, which thou knowest not."

KJV.

GOD'S UNIVERSAL PURPOSE FOR ALL TALENTS

There is a universal purpose for every talent God has given to man. In the book of Revelation 4:11; it is written,

"Thou art worthy, O Lord, to receive glory and honour and power: for thou
hast created all things, and for thy pleasure they are and were created." (KJV).

God created all things including man and every other thing he put in him (talent inclusive) for His pleasure. Awesome!!!

"If He is not entertained and satisfied, you have lost it". Your talent from the raw state to the period of development to the finished product should please God. Everything you do with your talent should put a smile on His face. The universal purpose for you being talented as an architect, doctor, singer, sportsman, make-up artist, engineer, etc., is to glorify and please Him. "For His pleasure" means for His enjoyment and satisfaction. If He is not entertained and satisfied, you have lost it. It then means you are

glorifying the devil with your talent, and your final destination is hell.

GOD'S INTENTION FOR TALENT

"Each one should use whatever gift he has received to serve others, faithfully administering God's grace in its various forms." 1 Peter 4:10 NIV.

God has given you unique abilities, talents and gifts, and these are what set you apart from the next person. Whether you are a cook, hairdresser, lecturer, etc.

God gave you those talents to serve others. Remember His word says each one, including you, should use whatever gift you have received to serve others. The fact is when you use your talent to serve others, God is satisfied and glorified. Much more than this, He said when we minister (serve) to others, we are actually doing it to Him. I don't know if you have seen God before. I have not! If you have, please show me where He is. People think that giving to God alone is when you bring money or things and drop it in church. The most effective and important way of giving to God is giving or ministering (serving) to someone.

"If you think your talents are simply for you to make a lot of money, retire and die, you've missed the point of your life. God gave you talents to benefit others, not

Rick Warren wrote in his Daily Hope devotional article on "Make the most of your talents" – If you think your talents are simply for you to make a lot of money, retire and die, you've missed the point of your life. God gave you talents to benefit others, not yourself and God gave other people talents that benefit you.

Our Lord Jesus gave this understanding in a story He told in Matthew 25:31-40.

"When the Son of man shall come in His glory, and all the holy angels with Him, then shall He sit upon the throne of glory; and before Him shall be gathered all nations; and He shall separate them one from another; as a shepherd divide His sheep from the goats: and he shall set the sheep on His right hand, but the goat on the left. Then shall the king say unto them on the right hand, come, ye blessed of my father, inherit the kingdom prepared for you from the foundation of the world; for I was an hungered, and ye gave me meat; I was thirsty, and ye gave me drink; I was a stranger, and ye took me in; naked, and ye clothed me; I was sick, and ye visited me; I was in prison, and ye came unto me. Then shall the righteous answer Him, saying, Lord, when saw we thee an hungered, and fed we thee? Or thirsty, and gave thee drink? When saw we thee a stranger, and took thee

in? Or naked, and clothed thee? Or when saw we thee sick, or in prison, and came unto thee? And the king shall answer and say unto them, verily I say unto you, inasmuch as ye have done it unto one of the least of these my brethren, ye have done it unto me."

The emphasis is on verse 40, which says:
And the king shall answer and say unto them, verily I say unto you, inasmuch as ye have done it unto one of the least of these my brethren, ye have done it unto me."

When we use our talent to serve humanity and make the world a better place, we are serving God and it is for His pleasure.

Bob Marley, an unbeliever, used his talent in music to fight for the independence of Zimbabwe and also stopped political violence in his country, Jamaica. Now, that is serving humanity. We need to use our talent to heal this world and make it a better place.

I have seen music ministers who are gifted singers, who lead praise and worship in churches and release albums to God's glory but are not solving any problem in the society with their gift. What ill in the society are you fighting against with your talent.

NOTE: If you are not serving

"We need to use our talent to make this world a better place".

humanity with your talent, there is a tendency for you to be selfish with it and pride will set in. There is no in-between. If you are not serving God with your talent, you will surely serve the devil with it. For example; most well-known talented comedians make the world laugh at their dirty immoral jokes. That's not healthy at all. The question is: for us to laugh must the joke be dirty? The giver of your talent (God) does not find pleasure in those dirty jokes. So you are not serving Him with your talent that way. I know of a very funny comedian who is entertaining a lot of people with clean and healthy jokes.

Note that every talent is important. None is insignificant. The Bible confirms this in Romans 12:6-8

In His grace, God has given us different gifts for doing certain things well. So if God has given you the ability to prophesy, speak out with as much faith as God has given you. If your gift is serving others, serve them well. If you are a teacher, teach well. If your gift is to encourage others, be encouraging. If it is giving, give generously. If God has given you leadership ability, take the responsibility seriously. And if you have a gift for showing kindness to others, do it gladly.

GOD'S EXPECTATION OF US

God sees us as stewards of the talents He has given to us. A steward is a caretaker and a manager of the talent God has given to him. Your talent may be great or small in your eyes, but they are relevant and important to God. The Bible says:

Now, a person who is put in charge as a manager must be faithful. 2 Corinthians 4:2. NLT.

God has given us talents to manage and He expects us to grow the talent and use it to His glory. He demands faithfulness from us. If you use your talent, it will grow. If you don't, you will lose it.

"There is no in-between. If you are not serving God with your talent, you will surely serve the devil with it"

TALENT AND CHARACTER

Talent is a gift but character is a choice-John C. Maxwell

It is said that your gift can take you to the top, but character will sustain you there. Also, it is easier getting to the top than remaining there. The most important step to personal effectiveness and leadership

"If you use your talent, it will grow. If you do not, you will lose it.

is character development or what some may call capacity building. After discovering your gift, having a vision etc., if you have character defects, it could rubbish all you have achieved and rob you of that role model status which provides you a platform to influence your generation. A case study is Tiger Woods, the greatest golfer of his generation. This was a young man who at 21 years, had risen to the top as the highest earning sportsman alive. Also he won the greatest sportsman of the year on about two occasions. He had won several titles in golf more than any other person. He earned more money in adverts as a sports role model more than others. What a remarkable career he had. But in 2009, he was caught in a major scandal of cheating his wife by being in a relationship with another lady and up till 2011 he didn't win any other trophy. He was stripped of almost all his advert earnings, and he was no longer regarded as a role model. All that success came crashing down.

An example some of us can remember in Nigeria is what happened to a former Speaker of the House of Representatives, Chief Dimeji Bankole, a very young man with a promising career. After enjoying the paraphernalia as the number four citizen in Nigeria, he was docked in court for corruption.

"Character protects your talent."

Since then he has gone into oblivion. In anything you do in life, note that your character whether good or bad, will always come to play. If you don't consciously build a decent character, you can never become successful in that field. Notice that your gift when harnessed, will bring you to limelight. People will want to know how you were able to achieve greatness. If you are fraudulent, dishonest, quarrelsome etc., you will not earn respect and people will not want to associate with you.

There is a limit to the height you will get to in life if you lack integrity. This is irrespective of how talented you are. Character protects your talent. It is very important to note that you can never climb beyond the limits of your character. Great people are disciplined people. Samson in the book of Judges in the Bible was very talented and anointed by God, but lack of strength of character was his greatest undoing.

"You can never climb beyond the limits of your character."
John C. Maxwell

A profound statement in the Bible says:

A person without self-control is like a city with broken-down walls. (Proverbs 25:28 NLT)

This means when you lack self-control, you are defenceless and vulnerable. Know that talent is never enough. Highly talented people always tend to get carried away by the accolades they receive from people and forget to develop their character.

"When you lack self-control, you are defenseless and vulnerable".

For you to become a role model to people who appreciate your talent, you must pay attention to character building because **"Character is the firm foundation stone upon which one must build to win respect. Just as no worthy building can be erected on a weak foundation, so no lasting reputation worthy of respect can be built on a weak character."— R. C. Samsel**

HOW TO DEVELOP INTEGRITY AND STRENGTH OF CHARACTER

"Good character is more to be praised than outstanding talent. Most talents are to some extent a gift. Good character, by contrast, is not given to us. We have to build it piece by piece—by thought,

choice, courage and determination." -John Luther

Personal integrity is the quality of being honest with yourself and others, and living a life that is aligned with your moral principles, not just liberty. Developing personal integrity requires examining your beliefs and value system, and taking conscious steps to behave in ways that are consistent with your personal moral code. To be able to do this, the following steps may be helpful:

Good character is more to be praised than outstanding talent. Most talents are to some extent a gift. Good character, by contrast, is not given to us. We have to build it piece by piece—by thought, choice, courage and determination."
-John Luther

1. **Identify aspects of your behaviour that require change**
   Reflect on your interactions with others in the workplace, at home, and in social situations to determine specific areas in need of improvement. For example, if you are late for work every day and feel guilty about creating excuses for this behaviour, this may be an opportunity to develop greater personal integrity.

2. **Determine your reasons for not behaving with greater personal integrity**
   For example, you may be pushing unpleasant work tasks on to other employees instead of being honest with your boss about your inability to do the tasks. You may be afraid to admit to yourself or to your boss that you do not possess the right skills or that the job is not the right fit for you.

3. **Face the obstacles that weaken you to excuse yourself, lie or violate your moral code**
   Get involved in finding a more suitable use of your talents, facing your fears about how others may perceive you and/or seeking knowledge or counselling to address personal challenges and insecurities.

4. **Expect a trial and error process that requires persistent effort.**
   Assess your progress, as success and integrity are not destinations, but making some progress and going forward. Expect yourself to learn and strive daily toward your goals, always making progress.

5. **Develop your accountability.**
   Learn to admit when you've made a mistake and

apologize for it. If you were at least partly to blame for a bad situation, own up to your part in it instead of blaming others. If you admit that you've done something wrong, it's easier to be more honest and to avoid the same mistake in the future.

6.   **Enlist the help of others, as mentors.**
    The smiles and advice of colleagues, relatives and good friends, who know you well and have your best interest at heart, can assist your progress by providing objective feedback on a daily basis about the personal changes you are making.

God who is the author of life made it clear in the Bible in 2 Timothy 3:16, 17(NLT) that
"All scripture is inspired by God and is useful to teach us what is true and to make us realize what is wrong in our lives. It corrects us when we are wrong and teaches us to do what is right. God uses it to prepare and equip his people to do every good work."

This means that for us to develop a life of integrity, we must pay attention to the Word of God. Take an honest assessment of yourself, note your character weaknesses and begin to work on them or they can be your greatest obstacle to greatness. Note your character strengths and also begin to strengthen them.

In conclusion, a life of leadership and personal effectiveness can be viewed from an angle where a person discovers his gift, develops a conviction on that gift, which in turn makes him to generate a vision, which ignites a passion for every avenue to inspire people by using his gift to serve. All these *"Good success can only come in association and fellowship with God".* are being done while he pays serious attention to developing integrity and character worthy of emulation.

A final word of advice on all who long to be successful in life can be found in the greatest book ever written, (The Bible) in Joshua 1 verse 8 (NLT) which says;

"This Book of the law shall not depart out of your mouth, but you shall meditate on it day and night, that you may observe and do according to all that is written in it. For then you shall make your way prosperous, and then you shall deal wisely and have good success."

Good success can only come in association and fellowship with God.

7

LEADERSHIP AND YOUR TALENT

Leadership is a subject that has been discussed over the years and misunderstood in this part of the world. The general concept people have about leadership is that it is for a particular set of people. They believe that it is all about having a title or position. When you mention leadership, people's minds run to Presidents, Governors, C.E.Os.', General Overseers, etc.

This misconception has made it such that people don't walk into a bookshop to buy a leadership book. When people see a program entitled "leadership conference", they just look away believing it is not for them. This has kept a lot of people at a mediocre level, robbing many people of their success in life and keeping them underdeveloped and ineffective.

The truth of the matter is that leadership is a very important subject that affects every aspect of life and is a must study for all who want to be influential, successful and outstanding in their generation. Like the great leadership expert John C. Maxwell put it, "Everything rises and falls on leadership". Except you apply the principles of leadership, chances are that you will miss out on living a life of relevance and influence.

Let us start by dealing with the misconception surrounding the subject of leadership. Leadership can be defined as the ability to guide, direct or effectively influence people. John C. Maxwell sums it up this way "Leadership is influence; nothing more nothing less." The word 'INFLUENCE' is a major recurring decimal in the definition of leadership and it means the ability to affect someone's character, behaviour or belief especially by providing an example for them to follow, thereby winning their admiration. Leadership is not about titles.

Having defined leadership, you can see that everyone

"Everything rises and falls on leadership"
John C. Maxwell

is a leader including you. This can be buttressed by looking at the Bible. God is the greatest leader ever and He said in Genesis 1:26(NIV).

Then God said, "Let us make mankind in our image, in our likeness, so that they may rule over the fish in the sea and the birds in the sky, over the livestock and all the wild animals, and over all the creatures that move along the ground."

God being a leader created us in His own image and likeness. This means we are leaders just as He is.

There are points to note; every definition you come across in leadership has to do with people. It has to do with people development and capacity building to achieve a particular purpose or vision. For you to effectively do this, you have to win people over, attract them and earn their respect to lead them or have them follow you.

"Leadership is influence; nothing more nothing less
John C. Maxwell

Another point also is that when you are influencing people, you are a leader. If I influence you to change the course you wanted to study in the university, I have led you and someone who leads is a leader.

The big question is – what is the relationship between

your talent and leadership? What I am about to share with you now is mind blowing and if you can connect to it, you will never be the same again. It will start a positive revolution in your inside for greatness. If our nation can latch in on it, this country will begin a match towards greatness.

ROAD MAP TO THE STAFF

TALENT-YOUR MAJOR SOURCE OF INFLUENCE

The biggest attraction in the world is God. When God created the human being, he did something that made every human on earth to be attracted to Himself one way or the other. **Genesis 2:7(NIV)**

Then the LORD God formed man from the dust of the ground and breathed into his nostrils the breath of life, and the man became a living being.

This breath of God in man has made it such that no acquisition of man or anything in this life can satisfy man except God Himself. So we are forever attracted to Him. God then put a very little gift of Himself in every human being so that people can be attracted to each other because of that very little gift of Himself in us. That very little part is your gift/talent. Your talent is that very little gift of God in you.

THE NEXT BIGGEST ATTRACTION IN THE WORLD IS TALENT.

Talent attracts and that is a profound truth. Everything on earth today is a product of talent. Without talent, there can never be excellence, and excellence attracts. Go out to the streets and look around. Whenever you see anyone doing anything exceptional, people gather to watch. Take a stick, throw it up and catch it on your back. Do it many times in the street. Before you know it, a crowd has gathered to watch you. What are they watching? Talent (as little as that is). The next thing, you're asked to pay if you want to watch. – Talent is a money spinner. There is a magnetic force in talent that attracts anytime talent is in action.

The Burjel Arab which is the world's tallest sea based hotel in Dubai is a product of talent, designed by the best talented architects in the world. It is a tourist attraction, raking in billions of dollars annually. People all over the world are attracted to that edifice.

Millions of people were attracted all over the world to watch the late Michael

"There is a magnetic force in talent that attracts

Jackson sing because of talent. I believe you also can give thousands of examples of the picture I am trying to paint here. What attracts people to you the most is your talent. Oftentimes people wonder why a lot of people are crowding towards a particular person and not themselves. Check it, the person has discovered his talent and is developing and deploying it. You that people are not following or crowding around, you have not discovered yours. Your talent travels and reaches places you might never get to till you die. What is your talent doing in those places? It is influencing millions of people you may never see all your life.

America as a nation is a leader. Why is America so attractive? Why is it that everyone wants to be there? You go there, spend your money and they get richer. The reason is that America is a product of talent. They celebrate talent, and when talent is in action, excellence is the result. Things are done excellently in that country and excellence attracts. In a recent study, it has been discovered that there is a relationship between excellence and talent. For instance, the Wright brothers mentioned earlier lived and died hundreds of years ago, but their talent is still speaking and affecting lives till today. Every time you fly in an aeroplane you are being influenced by that gift.

The key to the success of America is making sure square pegs are put in square holes; likewise round pegs are put in round holes thereby guaranteeing excellent deliveries with passion unlike in our nation where just anyone can work anywhere. For instance, in Nigeria, a lawyer or an architect sits in a bank counting money.

Talent attracts because you are at your best anytime you are using it. The best in you tends to come out. When you are exhibiting your talent, there is an influence you are exerting on people. Something is happening to them. You are affecting them. That is why lots of people always find themselves falling in love with talented people. The truth is that it is not him/her they are falling in love with, it is the gift of God they are falling in love with.

TALENT AND SERVICE

Remember that showcasing your talent means serving your talent. Every opportunity to display your talent is an opportunity to serve people, and when you serve people, you influence them. The big question is; when people are

"Every opportunity to display your talent is an opportunity to serve people, and when you serve people, you influence them.

attracted to me, what do I do with them? If we serve our talent rightly to humanity, our world will be a better place. If everyone will discover, develop and serve with his talent to humanity, the world will change for good.

ANCIENT PRINCIPLE
Our Lord Jesus Christ said in Mark 10:42 - 43 (NLT)

So Jesus called them together and said, "You know that the rulers in this world lord it over their people, and officials flaunt their authority over those under them. But among you it will be different. Whoever wants to be a leader among you must be your servant."

Can you picture the problem with the political leaders of our nation? Leadership is about service. So your talent is a platform for you to provide leadership to your generation. Discover your talent, develop it, nurture it, serve it to your generation with good character and you are practising the purest form of leadership.

From the oldest book ever written – The Holy Bible, the ancient principle for leadership can be seen clearly. People and nations who have practised these principles have excelled and become great people and nations.

JOSEPH THE FIRST PRIME MINISTER OF EGYPT

Here we will examine this story in the Bible Genesis 37:5-11 (KJV)

"Your talent attracts people to you, so that you can guide, direct and affect them positively with character

One night Joseph had a dream, and when he told his brothers about it, they hated him more than ever. "Listen to this dream," he said. "We were out in the field, tying up bundles of grain. Suddenly my bundle stood up, and your bundles all gathered around and bowed low before mine!"

His brothers responded, "So you think you will be our king, do you? Do you actually think you will reign over us?" And they hated him all the more because of his dreams and the way he talked about them.

Soon Joseph had another dream, and again he told his brothers about it. "Listen, I have had another dream," he said. "The sun, moon, and eleven stars bowed low before me!"

"This time he told the dream to his father as well as to his brothers, but his father scolded him. "What kind of dream is that?" he asked. "Will your mother and I and your brothers actually come and bow to the

ground before
you?" But while his brothers were jealous of Joseph,
his father wondered what the dreams meant.

In Ancient Egypt, a seventeen year old boy named Joseph had dreams. He could tell that this dream was not an ordinary dream. He understood it was a given talent. Though we were not told, but it can be deduced that this young man may have been having other dreams. God showed him things to come through the gift of dreams and their interpretation. Some of us do have disjointed dreams that mean nothing after heavy plates of garri in the night like myself, while some people's dreams come to pass, which is a gift.

Reading further in subsequent verses and chapters of that book (Genesis 37), Joseph had a lot of challenges and obstacles which are natural for any individual who is conscious of his talent and destiny. But he wouldn't let them discourage him. Like I mentioned in the last chapter, character is the foundation of leadership. It is the foundation that will sustain you at the top where your talent will obviously take you to. So for Joseph to become that successful leader, he needed to develop his talent and character. It is important to state here that the Ancient Principle for contemporary leadership states that before you receive the Staff, you must pass the all-important integrity test. Joseph's character had to be tested for God to use him to affect a nation and bring about His will to be done on earth. The story continues in Genesis 39: 6 -12(NLT)

So Potiphar gave Joseph complete administrative responsibility over everything he owned. With Joseph there, he didn't worry about a thing—except what kind of food to eat! Joseph was a very handsome and well-built young man, and Potiphar's wife soon began to look at him lustfully. "Come and sleep with me," she demanded.

But Joseph refused. "Look," he told her, "my master trusts me with everything in his entire household. No one here has more authority than I do. He has held back nothing from me except you, because you are his wife. How could I do such a wicked thing? It would be a great sin against God."

"She kept putting pressure on Joseph day after day, but he refused to sleep with her, and he kept out of her way as much as possible. One day, however, no one else was around when he went in to do his work. She came and grabbed him by his cloak, demanding, "Come on, sleep with me!" Joseph tore himself away, but he left his cloak in her hand as he ran from the house.

He took the test and because he did not compromise as you can read in subsequent verses, it landed him in prison. He was imprisoned but the gift of a man cannot be imprisoned, for the Bible says in Proverbs **18:16** (KJV)

A man's gift maketh room for him, and bringeth him before great men.

In this story, observe the very next thing the Bible had to say the moment Joseph was thrown into prison: Genesis 39:19 - 23 *(NLT)*

Potiphar was furious when he heard his wife's story about how Joseph had treated her. So he took Joseph and threw him into the prison where the king's prisoners were held, and there he remained. But the LORD was with Joseph in the prison and showed him his faithful love. And the LORD made Joseph a favourite with the prison warden. Before long, the warden put Joseph in charge of all the other prisoners and over everything that happened in the prison. The warden had no more worries, because Joseph took care of everything. The LORD was with him and caused everything he did to succeed.

We can deduce the following;

> Joseph recognized he had a talent
> He was developing his talent
> He was building a strong character

He passed the integrity test
Favour of God is released
God appeared powerfully on the scene and took
  over his affairs

While in prison an ancient principle that says
ALWAYS BE READY AND CAPITALIZE ON
EVERY OPPORTUNITY TO SERVE YOUR GIFT
was applied by Joseph. Be ready at all times. Don't
hide your gift. A wise man said," serve your talent
like a wealthy man spending his money till you go
broke."

In Genesis 40, this story continues with two people
from the palace of Pharaoh joining Joseph in prison
and they had dreams that troubled them. Joseph saw
their countenance and inquired of them;

*And they said unto him, we have dreamed a dream,
and there is no interpreter of it. And Joseph said unto
them, do not interpretations belong to God? Tell me
them, I pray you.*

Joseph reminded them that God is the giver of talent
and that God is omniscient. Finally they told him and
he served his gift free of charge by interpreting their
dreams without demanding anything. When you serve
people free, they tend to feel they are indebted to you.
Of course everything happened exactly as Joseph told

him. The man was restored to his position in the palace as the Chief Butler and when a similar situation played up with the Pharaoh being troubled about his dream, he quickly remembered and told Pharaoh about Joseph.

Genesis 41:14-16 (NLT)
Pharaoh sent for Joseph at once, and he was quickly brought from the prison. After he shaved and changed his clothes, he went in and stood before Pharaoh. 15 Then Pharaoh said to Joseph, "I had a dream last night, and no one here can tell me what it means. But I have heard that when you hear about a dream you can interpret it. 16 "It is beyond my power to do this," Joseph replied. "But God can tell you what it means and set you at ease."

Joseph was bold to declare that God is the source of his talent. When you go about the business of your talent, it announces you in places you never dreamt of. Imagine the President sending for you because of your talent.

Recognize this will not happen if you are doing nothing about your talent. Your talent was given to you to solve a problem as you can see with Joseph. What happened to him fulfils what the Bible says in Proverbs **18:16** (KJV)

A man's gift maketh room for him, and bringeth him before great men.

The dream had to do with the future of Egypt as a nation. Is it not interesting to note that the solution to a nation's problem and the future of a nation lies in the gift of God in a man/woman. Joseph served with his gift before Pharaoh by interpreting the dream. For pharaoh, he had done the extraordinary which is a bye-product of gift because none of his wise men who obviously didn't have the gift of interpreting dreams could do that. Note that anyone who has developed his gift will always be presented with an opportunity to serve with that gift and become great. This led to his appointment as the second-in-command to Pharaoh. Here is Joseph leading with his gift. His gift led to his appointment and brought him to a place of authority and influence over millions of people and took him through the road to his staff. Joseph also had the gift of administration, which he started using for the benefit of the nation. Let us take a look at Pharaoh's declaration after Joseph's interpretation of the dream;
Genesis 41:39-43
Then Pharaoh said to Joseph, "Since God has revealed the meaning of the dreams to you, clearly no one else is as intelligent or wise as you are. [40] You

will be in charge 40 of my court, and all my people will take orders from you. Only I, sitting on my throne, will have a rank higher than yours."

Pharaoh said to Joseph, "I hereby put you in charge of the entire land of Egypt." Then Pharaoh removed his signet ring from his hand and placed it on Joseph's finger. He dressed him in fine linen clothing and hung a gold chain around his neck. Then he had Joseph ride in the chariot reserved for his second-in-command. And wherever Joseph went, the command was shouted "Kneel down!" So Pharaoh put Joseph in charge of all Egypt. And Pharaoh said to him, "I am Pharaoh, but no one will lift a hand or foot in the entire land of Egypt without your approval."

See where talent can place a man. The same was the case in the book of Daniel with the four Hebrew boys, most especially, Daniel. He passed through almost the same sequence as Joseph. Let us also use that as a case study:

"When you go about the business of your talent, it announces you in"

DANIEL THE GOVERNOR

Daniel was one of the Hebrew children who

"Your talent was given to you to solve a problem".

was taken into exile after King **Nebuchadnezzar** of Babylon came to Jerusalem and besieged it. Just like Joseph, Daniel was a gifted child as was reported in the Bible in Daniel 1: 3-4 (NLT).

Then the king ordered Ashpenaz, his chief of staff, to bring to the palace some of the young men of Judah's royal family and other noble families, who had been brought to Babylon as captives. "Select only strong, healthy, and good-looking young men," he said. "Make sure they are well versed in every branch of learning, are gifted with knowledge and good judgment, and are suited to serve in the royal palace. Train these young men in the language and literature of Babylon."

In these verses you can see the first two deductions made earlier being mentioned. Daniel is gifted, and he was passed through training to develop his talent. The next is for him to build his character and develop integrity.

Daniel 1:5-8 (KJV)

And the king appointed them a daily provision of the king's meat, and of the wine which he drank: so nourishing them three years, that at the end thereof they might stand before the king. Now among these were of the children of Judah, Daniel, Hananiah, Mishael, and Azariah: Unto whom the prince of the eunuchs gave names: for he gave unto Daniel the name of Belteshazzar; and to Hananiah, of Shadrach; and to Mishael, of Meshach; and to Azariah, of Abednego. But Daniel purposed in his heart that he would not defile himself with the portion of the king's meat, nor with the wine which he drank: therefore he requested of the prince of the eunuchs that he might not defile himself.

King **Nebuchadnezzar**'s kingdom was a fetish one, and the food offered to Daniel and others were those sacrificed to their gods. Daniel knew this and purposed in his heart not to eat the food. It was a test of his character. He passed the test and the next step is that God released His favour upon him just as He did in the case of Joseph. This can be seen in the preceding verse.

Daniel 1:9 (KJV)
Now God had brought Daniel into favour and tender love with the prince of the eunuchs

Also because God gifted him, he worked hard and appreciated God as his source such that in very assessment made, Daniel was found to be exceptional and wiser compared to others.

Daniel 1:17-20
As for these four children, God gave them knowledge and skill in all learning and wisdom: and Daniel had understanding in all visions and dreams. Now at the end of the days that the king had said he should bring them in, then the prince of the eunuchs brought them in before Nebuchadnezzar. And the king communed with them; and among them all was found none like Daniel, Hananiah, Mishael, and Azariah: therefore stood they before the king. And in all matters of wisdom and understanding that the king enquired of them, he found them ten times better than all the magicians and astrologers that were in all his realm.

It happened that later in the story that the King had a disturbing dream. He demanded that his wise men told him both the dream and its interpretation. Of course that was an impossible thing to ask for, but remember that the gift of God has answers both to the impossible and the problem of any nation. Daniel by divine intervention, downloaded the dream and its interpretation and was brought before the King to bail out the entire nation. You see Daniel towing the same line and saying the same things Joseph said.

Then Arioch brought in Daniel before the king in haste, and said thus unto him, I have found a man of the captives of Judah, that will make known unto the king the interpretation. The king answered and said to Daniel, whose name was Belteshazzar, Art thou able to make known unto me the dream which I have seen, and the interpretation thereof? Daniel answered in the presence of the king, and said, the secret which the king hat demanded   cannot the wise men, the astrologers, the magicians, the soothsayers, shew unto the king; But there is a God in heaven that revealeth secrets, and maketh known to the king Nebuchadnezzar what shall be in the latter days. Thy dream, and the visions of thy head upon thy bed, are these;

As for thee, O king, thy thoughts came into thy mind upon thy bed, what should come to pass hereafter: and he that revealeth secrets maketh known to thee what shall come to pass. But as for me, this secret is not revealed to me for any wisdom that I have more than any living, but for their sakes that shall make known the interpretation to the king, and that thou mightest know the thoughts of thy heart .

Daniel stood before the King and boldly declared that his source was God. After he told the King the dream and its interpretation, the Bible recorded that the King bowed to Daniel.

Daniel 2: 46-48

Then King Nebuchadnezzar threw himself down before Daniel and worshiped him, and he commanded his people to offer sacrifices and burn sweet incense before him. [47] The king said to Daniel, "Truly, your God is the greatest of gods, the Lord over kings, a revealer of mysteries, for you have been able to reveal this secret." [48] Then the king appointed Daniel to a high position and gave him many valuable gifts. He made Daniel ruler over the whole province of Babylon, as well as chief over all his wise. At Daniel's request, the king appointed Shadrach, Meshach, and Abednego to be in charge of all the affairs of the province of Babylon, while Daniel remained in the king's court.

Can you imagine how gift can make a President to bow and worship his subject? That is the power of what you carry in your inside. You see how people are riding on the wings of talent to prominence and leadership. The same can also be said of David in the Bible. It is truly an ancient principle.

CONCLUSION

We have unravelled a mystery which has been neglected by developing countries in Africa like our nation Nigeria. The solution to our problem lies in our discovering, nurturing and deploying our gifts. The gift of God in us, makes the impossible possible. Just like we read, if we all can pay attention to the principles in this book, our relevance will become so pronounced that governments will begin to look unto us for the solution to the problem of our States. This can only be done accurately when we acknowledge the author and finisher of our faith (Jesus Christ).

In conclusion, The Coin and The Staff will not be complete without letting you know that when you recognize and acknowledge God who is the source of your gift, the Holy Spirit will empower your gift and the sky becomes your stepping stone to greater heights. Acknowledging Him in your life means accepting Jesus as your Lord and Saviour. The Bible says in Romans 10:10 (KJV)

For with the heart, man believeth unto righteousness; and with the mouth confession is made unto salvation.

This means that the steps towards salvation include the following;

- Believe in your heart that Jesus is God made manifest in the flesh.
- That He died for your sins.
- Acknowledge you are a sinner.
- Confess your sins and repent.
- Accept and confess Him as your Lord and Saviour.

Once you do these, you are born again. A new life has begun and old things are passed away.

2 Corinthians 5:17—*Therefore if any man be in Christ, he is a new creature:*
old things are passed away; behold, all things are become new. (KJV).

If you have not consciously done this you can repeat this prayer with belief in your heart.

Lord Jesus, today I recognize that I am a sinner, I confess my sins, forgive me and cleanse me with your blood. I acknowledge that you died for me on the cross. I receive you now as my Lord and personal

Saviour. Thank you for saving me, thank you because I am born again.

Congratulations and welcome to the family of God.